CW01018040

NO ONE INVITED ME
AND SO I THREW MY OWN!

In loving memory of my dad, Derrick Holdsworth (1932–2009).

NO ONE INVITED ME AND SO I THREW MY OWN!

Grit

Originally submitted in 2008.
In the 'Year of the Mask' (2020)
a lot of this has never been more apt!

ARTHUR H. STOCKWELL LTD
Torrs Park, Ilfracombe, Devon, EX34 8BA
Established 1898
www.ahstockwell.co.uk

British Library Cataloguing-in-Publication Data.
A catalogue record for this book is available
from the British Library.

By the same author:
Natural Woman
Maybe Another Time When I'm Not Watching TV!

ISBN 978-0-7223-3970-1
Printed in Great Britain by
Arthur H. Stockwell Ltd
Torrs Park   Ilfracombe
Devon EX34 8BA

Contents

OUT ON THE TOWN

I know, you know, we all know
She'll have a really good time
Cos she's got panache,
Cos she's wearing her glad rags,
Cos she's got a lot to tell,
Cos she's got the rhythm in her,
Cos she's holding her head high,
Cos she always comes up smiling,
Cos she always has the last laugh . . .

(UN)CULTIVATED

Well educated
with no common sense.
Well educated
with no scruples.
Well educated
with no feel for money.
Well educated
with no urge to connect with others (unless they do).
Well educated
with no inclination to give (to anyone!).

DWELLING PLACE

Home is where the heart is.
Mine's here cos that's where
it's beating (rhythmically).
Frank S. left his in San Francisco.
Just where is yours pulsating?

IN TWO MINDS

I saw you.
Did you see me?
I was surprised (pleasantly).
Were you?
I blushed.
Did you?
I was longing.
Were you?
I was close to tears.
Were you?
I was torn.
Were you?
Between staying (in that queue)
and leaving (to follow you),
Between staying in town
and leaving to share once more my bed (with you),
Between staying together all Sunday
and you not leaving at all,
Are we thinking alike?

ENGAGED

I have a ring on my finger.
I can't get through.
I'm busy.
I'm taken.
I'm hired.
I'm in thought.
I'm enchanted.
I'm in a battle of strength or words.
I'm talking.
I'm switched on.
I'm enlisted.
I'm reserved.
I'm preoccupied.
I'm spoken for.

ALTERNATIVES

"You might fall between the chairs," she said.
And I did.
A constant state.
Couldn't land a proper job.
Had no options (so how could I give you any?).
Didn't have 'all the chances', which is what
I was once led to believe.
I'm in no-man's-land
most of the f - - - - - - time.
Refusal after refusal.
Worst case is no reply.
Yet another form to be signed, sealed and delivered.
An additional brick wall to chip away at.
More boulders to roll aside.
How sweet it is to be (loved) challenged!

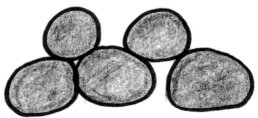

END OF DAY

When it comes to data,
It's final,
It's completed,
It's concluded,
It's closed,
It's gone through,
It's expired,
It's shut down,
It's n.a.i.p. – no additional input practicable –
It's logging out,
Rien de va plus!

DESERTER

For your sake:
Sorry for absconding, my brother.
Sorry for abandoning you, my cousin.
Sorry for leaving you high and dry, my friends.
Sorry for vacating my bedroom, Mum and Dad.
Sorry for defecting, my fatherland.
But it had to be done –
for my sake!

WOMANLY

It's female.
It's being feminine.
It's acting ladylike.
It's being matronly.
It's motherly.
It's being tender and warm.

} *Now & Then*

But, in addition,
It's exercising power.
It's being a vamp.
It's sporty.
It's being decisive.
It's wearing the trousers. . . .

} *Now*

15

SALOME IN REVERSE

She wanted John's head.
He wants mine.
His was on a platter.
Mine will be in a plastic bag.
Sign of the times.
What do they have in common?
Blinding jealousy!

WONDER DRUG

To be taken 1–3 times a day,
Alternatively when in need.
Before or after a meal.
With or without water.
It can medicate, knock out, stupefy,
numb, anaesthetise, poison, deaden, treat.

It's amazing, extraordinary, miraculous,
sensational, unique, rare.
They don't give it to just anyone.
It's the remedy and it's phenomenal.
It's being on a constant high.
You're in heaven but on earth
when you're in possession of it.
So just take me.

SIGNED, SEALED AND DELIVERED

At long last it's on the dotted line.
Free of our (your) debt!
Mismanagement for the most part.
Now you're sat there with the lot –
the *activa*, the *passiva*.
Could have had this in the bag much sooner.
I had to pay for it first though.
For being a bag – which I wasn't!

NORWEGIAN

N – northern abode when it comes to the map of the world.

O – orderly when it comes to house and garden.

R – reserved when it comes to one's nature.

W – wary when it comes to foreigners.

E – energetic when it comes to winter sports.

G – generous when it comes to charity (national and international).

I – implicit when it comes to what they actually think.

A – antagonistic when it comes to joining the EU.

N – nitpicking when it comes to choice of partner.

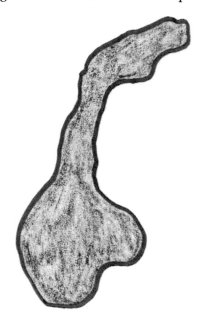

NOTHING PLANNED

I'm the 'life and soul' of the party.
But no one invited me!
So I threw my own.
The Chardonnay was flowing.
The pasta was swimming
in a creamy sauce with prawn.
The cake was chocolaty.
The fireworks, by courtesy of a large
part of the community, were amazing.
The music was tremendous, with renditions
by Elton John, live from Caesars Palace;
Kylie Minogue, live from London; and
yours truly, live from Gjøvik.
And the party outfit was really quite stunning –
a lot of black with a touch of diamanté and gold.
And for once I looked like I had a cleavage –
a sight which could have enchanted just
about any man in the place, if only there'd been one!
Who knows what this next year will bring!
Well, if it started as it means to go on,
I suppose I'll be wining and dining *chez moi*.
And I'd better get some mothballs for
those tight trousers and that sexy top, seeing
as they won't be seeing much light of day!

TRIALS AND TRIBULATIONS

Make sure you keep yourself alive.
And if it's getting that 'wonder potion',
that's the answer, then –
GO FOR IT!
Whatever it takes or costs.
That's an order!
Cos I don't want to be arranging
flowers for you yet.

PRIVATE VIEWING

How about you showing me your

* Collection of stamps,
* Album of faraway places,
* Selection of tunes,
* Accumulation of bestsellers,
* Choice of tipple,
* Store of savoury nibbles,
* Compendium of games,
* Assortment of favourite positions.

PICK AND CHOOSE

Some people seem to think that I'm
attracted to every man I see or speak to!
That's really quite wrong.
There is only a handful of men I'm truly interested in.
There's just one thing, though:
they think they are 'God's gift to women'
(and probably are), or
they are 'loaded' and show off about it in the
most boring way, or
they aren't interested in sex or any kind of
contact with a woman, or
they are just too egocentric for words, or
they are only half my age and others
can't handle it.
How positively irritating!

I ♥ NYC

They scrape the sky,
Each one taller than the other;
And, for as far as the eye can see,
They block the sunlight.
They cool down.
They captivate the tourist eye.
Been there, done that –
Done it all really!
Know NYC like the back of my hand.
'After Eight' in the subway only at your own risk.
Otherwise the only thing you don't do is walk on red.
You can shop 'til you drop if you like.
It's worth spending Time in the Square.
A musty smell, although it's not that long
since those Englishmen found New England!
Behind a splendid facade, rodent wallowing in filth.
A wave of yellow and the steaming holes.
A constant buzz.
Still, I slept in the city that never does.

I usually prefer oranges to apples,
But I love this big one.

MAKING A DIFFERENCE

You're lovely!
What does that mean?
Is it sharing a hard-boiled egg?
Is it almost breaking your neck
not to keep someone waiting?
Is it wearing pretty clothes?
Is it cooking a four-course meal
for three when you're dead on your feet?
Is it risking your life for someone
you don't know from Adam?
Is it walking around with a smile on your face
when you've got the whole world on your shoulders?
Is it helping others when you're actually
the one in need?
Is it doing things no one in their wildest
dreams would expect of you?
Yes, this is what it means.

HELLO AND GOODBYE (a)

Hi, **babe**.
Bye, son.

Hello, my dear.
See you, **buster**.

Ciao, darling.
Go for it, Mum.

Salut, my friend.
Bye-bye, **sweetie**.

Move over, **gorgeous**.
Call me, handsome.

Greetings, princess.
So long, **lad**.

Good day, boss.
Take care, nipper.

Get you, muscleman.
Ta-ra, love.

HELLO AND GOODBYE (b)

Harry:
Look at that **babe** over there! I believe she's **Buster's** new conquest.
He's certainly gonna **go** overboard to keep her, I bet.
Heard she's a right **sweetie**. And – guess what? –
She has this absolutely **gorgeous** sister!
I'm gonna **go** crazy big time if I don't get her number and give her a **call** sometime soon.

Guy:
Calm down, **lad**! You're going red in the face.
I'd better **get you** a glass of iced water, hey?

**B AND T
(Beautiful and Tempted –
in Her Eyes)**

You were beautiful.
You were tempted.
We were so together and bewitched.
And now?
Bored and tormented!

TWENTY QUESTIONS

I'd like to get to know you better.
So:
Have you ever worn women's underwear?
Have you been to Brighton?
Have you seen the film *Apocolypse Now*?
Do you know how to make dumplings?
Do you know the German word for black?
Did you suck on a dummy when you were a baby?
How many odd socks do you have?
What makes you cry?
Do you like *Last Night of the Proms*?
Do you prefer it on the back seat of a car
or in the woods?
Who is your favourite supermodel?
Can you juggle?
Would you do a bungee jump if asked?
What was Henry VIII's first wife called?
Do you like mussels in a white-wine sauce?
Do you like to French kiss?
Where do you work out?
Which cut of jeans do you prefer?
Do you have a dollar bill?
What would you think about if
death was staring you in the face?

SPECTACULAR

Fountains of light.
Rockets shooting off into the night.
Sporadic explosions of bright.
All this above a sea of white.
How magnificent the sight!
To stand in awe at this was so right.
Finished with the culinary bite.
Heavy with sleepiness to stay awake, I fight.
But now dreaming of what's to come
and my eyes at long last fastened tight.

HOME ALONE
ON NEW YEAR'S EVE

Not Kevin home alone but Jill.
I'm ringing it all in
with my wine and tele(vision) – the good at least.
The bad and the ugly I'd care to forget –
The good still to come,
the bad that's gone and
the ugly that still accompanies me.
The former I welcome with open arms,
the next is nothing but a consolation, and
the latter I'm sick and tired of.

CHEERS!

Here's to you –
whoever you are,
wherever you are,
whatever your passion;
whoever you're with,
where you're doing it,
whatever that is(!).
Why aren't you here
doing it with me?

MOTHER LOVE

Yes, I'm angry every day because

 I cherish,

I tend,

I nurture,

I protect,

I fight for,

I accompany,

I humour,

I entertain,

I spoil,

I raise - you, my little s o n e

PS It's all part and parcel of it –

Gifts for the future.

BATMAN

If you were a little less stupid, you would
speak to me, listen to me, understand me,
forgive me, stop crying, love me,
stay with me, share (water and wine) with me.

BITTERSWEET

As we're making love we

- can't get enough,
- can't breathe,
- can't talk,
- can't leave the sheets without red cheeks,
- can't catch a bite,
- can't believe the clock,
- can't say goodbye normally.

GOOD INVESTMENT

What's the point in spending so much on underwear
when all you want to do is rip it off?
Yes, but that's the fun of it:

* ripping it off(!),
* watching your face change,
* giving the garbage man something to
  think about – for days, weeks, months . . .
* having an excuse to buy a collection of new.

ONE ON ONE

Everybody needs someone:
    to love, to hate, to look at,
    to care for, to hold, to shout at,
    to kiss, to laugh with, to talk to,
    to cry with, to share with, to blame,
    to smile at, to argue with,
    to hold hands with, to criticise,
    to sing to, to dress up for,
    to go for walks in the forest with,
    to enjoy the sea and the sun with,
    to make candlelit dinners for,
    to dance the night away with,
    to open up to . . .

GREY MATTER

God gave me mine to use!
What do you have yours for?
He had his thoroughly washed.
She had hers picked far too often.
He thinks he's got a super one.
She was told hers resembles a pea.
He's sat on his most of the time.
Hers often gives off waves. . . .

YEARS

It's his day today –
Already so capable,
But still so much to learn.
Six gone, now into the seventh,
and many more to come:
Wonderful ones, painstaking ones,
Exciting ones, worrying ones,
Precious ones, damn-hard-work ones,
Never-to-be-forgotten ones, lonely ones,
Well-planned ones, chaotic ones,
Fun-packed ones, (none the) wiser ones.
I wish the **best ones** (of his life)
for him – always.

NOURISHMENT

"She's thirsty," they said mockingly.
"I'm hungry too," I say.
But I don't mean for food or drink.

Burger

I will not be quenched or fulfilled
until I have my teeth in your flesh,

Pizza

until I can lick the drops of perspiration
running down your back.

chips   kebab

You're not to be bought kilo-wise over the counter,
pre-packed from the fridge or to be ordered on the telephone.
You're free, and just about the tastiest dish
I've ever set my eyes on.

SOS

Mine was answered.
It turned my whole life around.
I needed it.
I don't mind acting the part of
a zombie, but not real time.
That's what I'd become:
No sparkle, no feelings.
"Mirror, mirror on the wall,
Who is the fairest one of all?"
It wasn't responding in my favour.
A hollow structure of a face was all I could see.
But crying for help is not easy.
I cried (buckets) eventually.
I was helped (lots).
Hopefully many more females
like me will be!

TO TEACH

What is that exactly?
To pass on knowledge,
To motivate,
To encourage,
To point in the right direction,
To foster creativity,
To challenge,
To question,
To criticise,
To test,
To actually hatch the next generation's
stars, decision-makers, leaders (spiritual or otherwise) . . .

`31-33-40`

Are these your measurements?
Or
Is it three friends between the age of thirty and forty-one?
Or
Are they three numbers out of the lotto?
Or
Are they the three worst times on the stopwatch
at a 5-km sponsored run?
Or
Is it the temperature in a well-known holiday
resort in Spain on three consecutive days?
Or
Is it really a car number plate?

Anyway, in case you're interested, mine are:
`32-24-32`

WHAT A DIFFERENCE THIRTY DAYS MAKES!

A month is a long time:
    to go on holiday,
    to wait for results,
    to give notice,
    to eat nothing but rice,
    to be on crutches,
    to be in a cage,
    to hunger (strike),
    to be in solitary,
    to sit by the phone,
    to long to see someone again.

OFF BALANCE

The never-ending pain of yearning:
    to see you (but not merely by
    chance/surprise or with masked faces),
    to be with you,
    to be read to by you (that voice so strong),
    to dance with you,
    to be held by you.
What torment!

A love so strong,
Every inch of my pale body aches – for you.
Dreams alone are not enough to cure.
Never before these feelings?
No, different, for no three people are alike on this earth.

That sweet smile once (1 ×) truly manifested,
not forgotten until my eyes one last time will close.
My ignorance of your kindness hangs over me –
why so immature?
I cannot answer for my foolish ways.
They were foolish, but led by excitement,
uncertainty and the fear of losing control.

For your eyes only are these words from my
heavy (not deceitful) heart.

AID AND ABET

Can I help you?
Maybe.
But with problems like mine
I need the big boys,
the bad boys,
the boys with the power to enforce,
the triple AAAs of this world,
the elite division,
the boys with the finger on the button . . .
Now tell me: do you qualify?

POWER!

FORCE!

44

DAD
(Dear and Devoted)

Maybe not as nimble and quick
as once you (and Jack) were,
But you're still 'the man'.
You've kicked, sliced and driven
some balls over the years.
You've knocked some people
into touch too.
A spade's a spade, right?
And that little piece of garden
is all the more pretty for you using one.
You're truly 'dear' to me and mine,
and you're totally 'devoted' to . . . my mum.

PENNIES FROM HEAVEN

Wish I had some of those.
The state has to give me most of mine right now.
Still, they let themselves be counted like any other –
Exact in colour, shape, size and feel.
They don't feel 'good', though.
Who cares? Me and mine have to exist.
Wells dry up, though.
Just hope this one doesn't –
not for now anyway.

ENGLISH

E – enduring when it comes to pain or cause.
N – nonchalant when it comes to change.
G – genteel when it comes to manners.
L – loyal when it comes to fellow humans.
I   – innovative when it comes to any form of art.
S – sentimental when it comes to memorabilia.
H – hated for having once been so great.

TACKLE

The nearest I got to fishing so far
was to buy a Barbour jacket –
Windproof, waterproof, bite-proof;
Big pockets for hooks, bait and hot-
water bottle to boot;
Zippers going in both directions
for quick access;
Inlets permit the body to respire air;
An oily feel;
Blends in well with nature;
Not usually worn by fishwives of a harsh kind.

BLACK HOLE

How I adore you!
And so you not speaking to me
Is sheer torture!
Don't feel myself,
But want to feel *you*
In every possible way:

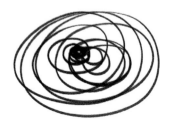

* around me,
* next to me,
* behind me,
* through the glass to me!

ANDREW'S CHOICE

Silk gloves, red lipstick, avocado, salmon, chardonnay, stockings, plastic trousers, hats and caps, fish and chips, Wedgwood, *Riverdance,* black stilettos, white roses, sounds of (rock) music, cream teas, short skirts, tickets to the ballet, iced coffee, French, jeans, corsets.

These are some of *my* favourite things, Julie.

PUNCTUALITY (AT ANY PRICE?)

"You're late, you're late,
you're late, you're late,
you're late, you're late,
you're late, you're late!"
He cried.

Sorry, I'm so sorry.
Embarrassment.
Why so angry?
I could have died on the way!
You couldn't know that!
Or was it just the unbearable desire
to see me turn that corner?

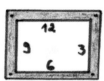

SAVOY

So you thought you were going
to stay at that exclusive hotel.
Well, you're not!
You're staying in a cultivated
kind of cabbage, having a compact
head and wrinkled leaves.
Have a pleasant stay.

Pay T.V.
Room Service
À la Carte
Minibar
Hair Salon
Fitness Centre

A NICE BREAK

When the sun shines in through the tiny windows,
One thinks of the sea and warmth;
Attractive to the eye the freshness of the walls so white;
Wonderful to get away for most;
The sand under the feet;
A tingling, a burning sensation in patches;
Wading in up to the knees, up to the waist, up over the
shoulders;
Heaven!
A well-earned break – a clean break, a final break –
before once more the routine sets in!

ONE THING LEADS TO ANOTHER

A bomb!
That explodes.
With anger, excitement or ecstasy?
Ecstasy - don't take those pills!
Kids keep going on the dance floor when they do.
Dance on a Saturday night at Chaplin.
Charlie **Chaplin** was a very funny man.
It's **funny** how Jordan rolls her eyes.
Eyes mirror the soul.
Both yours were beautiful.
How **beautiful** it is to be loved.
Love makes the world go round.
World peace.
Peace of mind.
Free your **mind** or else . . .
Mind what you do and say.
No, **do** what's in your **mind**!

LIFE AFTER BIRTH

No fear in the world could have stopped me from
bringing something so beautiful on to this harsh planet.

No mountain too high could have concealed
his uncompromising smile to me every morning.

Nine months of waiting – an eternity!

But, at long last, here before me lies my 'glittering prize'.

THE ULTIMATE ILLNESS

WWW stands for **W**orld **W**ide **W**eb – wrong!

Too easy, baby!

WWW stands for that slimy green animal
most good citizens choose not to acknowledge.
But it's there and it's LOUD and it won't go
away – not for a sad, long time.

Get real. WWW is **everyone's** problem –

That **W**orld **W**ide **W**orry!

GREAT ATTEMPT

So how did I do, then?
Was I better than last year?
Was my timing right?
Did you like my touch?
Do I compare (in a competitive sense)?
Would you like to come again (later)?
You said you were tired!
Did you think I gave my all?
Well, sorry, still have lots more to offer.
Bet you'd like to know how you scored, though.

PS: Will you be wanting to use my phone (also) again next try?

TO WEAR THE CROWN

"If I ruled the world . . ."
* they'd be out on the streets protesting,
* the phone lines would be burning night and day,
* the TV would bring non-stop disaster coverage,
* the radio would call for (deposition) votes via Freephone,
* they'd be queuing in their droves for one-way tickets to Mars.
Why?
Cos "she looks like mutton dressed as lamb" according to them.
Well, they'd have to find some excuse, wouldn't they!

MY WAY

It's just how I am with people:
I pick up when down,
I cause a smile,
I excite,
I radiate warmth,
I increase confidence,
I challenge,
I shock.
But, more important,
I make them the centre of attraction.
It's an ongoing project.

JOURNEY

You shake your head.
You don't get on the bus.
You shake your head.
You don't get on the bus.
You shake your head.
You don't get on the bus.
You shake your head.
You do♥get on the bus.
Does that mean this is the route
You are now ready to take?
Who knows where it might lead!
That's your fear –
It will take you to the land of no return.
A place so beautiful you will never want to leave.

CLEAR INDICATION

You have to show me L♥V !
Well, otherwise how do I know:
    if you truly like me,
    if you miss me,
    if you dream of me,
    if you lust for me,
    if you anticipate spending any whatsoever
    (quality) fun time with me,
    if you dare to take a chance (of a lifetime) with me?

REWARD

He got a bottle of red wine for his idea.
What do I get for mine?
Frowned upon,
Laughed at,
Picked on,
Cheated.

But then:
Admiration,
Respect,
Enthusiasm.

Applause.

As one says in Norwegian: B A R E *A* = Just *A*!

MY MUM

My mum is my mum and always will be.
Whatever the weather,
Wherever I am (far or near),
However I'm feeling (down or up),
Whatever I'm doing (wrong or right),
Whoever I'm with (or on my own),
She's always here (or there) for me.
And I adore her for it.
Mummy,♥ ma,♥ mom,♥ dam,♥ . . .

THREE BY FOUR

Roses are red,
Violets are blue,
Chocolate cake is ace
And so are you.

Roses are red,
Violets are blue,
Wonder how you'd react
if I said I loved you too.

Roses are red,
Violets are blue,
Put your arms around my neck
cos I so adore you.

MY COLOUR SCHEME

Red for the brash.
Blue for the sad and lonely.
Grey for the not-out-of-the-ordinary.
Purple for the royal.
Black for the stylish and aloof.
Orange for the tropical.
Pink for the 'sugar 'n spice and all things nice'.
White for the not-so-naive-after-all.
Yellow for the bright.
Green for the one in camouflage.
Brown for the dark and morbid.

CREATURE

Scorpions are the most beautiful creatures around.
Once captured by one, you won't (want to) get away.
How wonderful such feeling of uncontrollable desire,
rendered motionless and incomparable yearning
felt by its captive!